THE
CHRISTIAN
MANIFESTO

THE CHRISTIAN MANIFESTO

A Provocative Perspective on
Protestantism

Dr. T.F. Lewis

Lady Wisdom
Winter Park, FL

Paperback ISBN 978-0-9893151-9-7
E-book ISBN 978-0-9893151-8-0
Book cover design by: 1106 Design, LLC, www.1106design.com
Editing and interior design by: Tanya Brockett,
www.HallagenInk.com

Printed in the USA

Contents

Introduction

I wrote this book for everyone who desires to gain insight into what it means to be "a real Christian."

It seems that nowadays, a lot of people have misconceptions regarding Christianity, both believers and non-believers alike. A lot of non-believers I have come into contact with think that Christians are supposed to be perfect, and so when they see a Christian sin, they prove to themselves that being a Christian is either "too hard" or not worthwhile because Christians are hypocrites.

Yes, many great Christian leaders have fallen from grace over the past several decades, and indeed this is troubling and disheartening. In fact, the Bible says it is better to kill yourself than lead someone else down the wrong path or cause them to lose their faith (Luke 17:2, Mark 9:42). But because no man is infallible, we are not to look at mankind to see how to live our best lives. Rather, we are to look at Christ's example of perfect living in the Bible to guide our actions.

Many Christians with whom I've come into contact believe that it is their job to tell everyone else what they are doing wrong. This isolates them on their high horses and repels others rather than drawing them closer. The truth is that all of us have sinned and fallen short of the standards God wants us to live up to (see Romans 3); and that none of us are fit to judge another (unless we want to jeopardize our ability to receive mercy from God, see Matthew 7).

During the Casey Anthony trial (which I will discuss later in further detail), I realized that I, even though a born-again Christian, could be quite judgmental and lack compassion. After a revelation I had during the trial, I began to ask myself:

- "What does it mean to be a real Christian?"
- "What qualities should Christians possess?"
- "What are our moral duties and obligations?"
- "What other things am I doing that I shouldn't be?"
- "What should we avoid doing so as to be witnesses for God as opposed to hypocrites to the world who is watching us so carefully?"

I will warn you now that while the first half of the book is an overview of the basic principles of Christianity, the final half may be viewed as "radical," "progressive," "provocative," or worse; but I am answering the aforementioned questions with information directly found in the Bible with references included. The particular version of the Bible used is also noted. While it may seem like this manuscript is laden with scripture, this is intentional—I find that the best way to prove a point regarding Christianity is to demonstrate it through scriptural references.

While I am child of two pastors and have been in church my entire life, I am *not* a pastor, and I don't hold a PhD in theology or divinity. I don't know it all, nor do I have it all together. By profession I am a physician; but more importantly, I am a Christian seeking to do better—to live the best, most Christ-centered and Christ-pleasing life I can live—and I desire to help both Christians and non-Christians alike to better understand what being a Christian really means.

Another objective of mine is to be a witness and minister to non-believers, so that they may join us in our faith. As I previously mentioned, I am no pastor, but I believe this book had to be written by a layman, because the general public frequently distrusts the clergy and feels they are hypocrites.

Consider the great Christian leaders and pastors who over the last several decades have been exposed in the media for being drug-addicts, whores, adulterers, murderers, and child-molesters. It is no wonder that church attendance is currently at an all-time low! Rather than being a light in a dark world, an antibiotic to cure hurting people, and leading people TO Christ, the church has been acting more like bacteria, inflicting more pain and disease, and leading people astray.

Now I am not suggesting that those who don't act "Christ-like," but have accepted Christ into their hearts are not truly saved, because they are. But what I am saying is that such people don't have the "Mind of Christ," and aren't therefore able to live the victorious lives God has called us to live. With that said, my final objective is to let people know that there *are* many *real* Christians (i.e., saved AND "Christ-like" people) out there, and that anyone who desires can be one too!

The Greatest Commandment

What We Believe

As Christians, we believe that Jesus is the Son of God and that He came to earth and lived a blameless life that we are to try our best to emulate. We believe that because of His perfect and immense love for us, He died for our sins so that we would not perish, but have the chance of living eternally with God in heaven if we accept Him into our hearts as our Lord and Savior (John 3:16). We also believe that He rose from the dead, and now sits at the right hand of God, and that

Jesus the Son, God the Father, and the Holy Spirit are One—the blessed Trinity. We believe that if anyone simply confesses their sins to God, turns from their sins, and accepts Jesus into their hearts, they will be "saved," and spend eternity with Him in heaven. These are the cornerstone beliefs of our faith.

How to be Christ-Like

So as "Christians," obviously we are supposed to be "like Christ," but how do we accomplish this? Well, 1 John 4:8 says that "God is love." It is important to point out that while in the English language, there is only one word for love, in the ancient Greek, there were three: *agape* (unconditional love), *phileo* (brotherly love), and *eros* (erotic/romantic love). The type of love referred to in this scripture is agape—the highest form of love.

The entire scripture starting with verse 7 to verse 11 says, "Dear friends, let us love one another, because love comes from God. Whoever loves is a child of God and knows God. Whoever does not love does not know God, for God is love. And God showed His love for us by sending His only Son into the world, so that we might have life through Him. This is what love is: it is not that we have loved God, but that He loved us and sent His Son to be the means by which our sins are forgiven. Dear friends, if this is how God loved us, then we should love one another" (*Good News Translation*, GNT).

Jesus, in John 15:12 says, "My commandment is this: love one another, just as I love you" (GNT). In John 13:34-35 Jesus further says, "And now I give you a new commandment: love one another. As I have loved you, so you must love one another. If you have love for one another, then everyone will know that you are my disciples" (GNT).

In Mark 12, Jesus was asked by a teacher what the greatest commandment was and He responded this way in verses 29 and 30, "The most important one is this: 'Listen, Israel! The Lord our God is the only Lord. Love the Lord your God with all your heart, with all your soul, with all your mind, and with all your strength.' The second most important commandment is this: 'Love your neighbor as you love yourself.' There is no other commandment more important than these two" (GNT).

The Bible also says in 1 Corinthians 14:1, "let love be your highest goal!" (New Living Translation, NLT), or in other words, "Go after a life of love as if your life depended on it—because it does" (*The Message*, MSG). I love how *The Message* translation of 1 Corinthians 13:13 says this, "But for right now, until that completeness, we have three things to do to lead us toward that consummation: Trust steadily in God, hope unswervingly, love extravagantly. And the best of the three is love." So I believe by looking at the scripture it is clear to see that if we want to be Christians ("like Christ"), then *our biggest mission in life should be to emanate, radiate, demonstrate, and extravagantly <u>love</u>—first God, and then others.*

Love

This naturally leads us to additional questions such as, "what is love, really?" "How do I show love?" "What is love *not*?" 1 Corinthians has a lot to say about love, and we can find many answers here. Let's first examine what love is not/what it does not do. 1 Corinthians 13 tells us this in verses 4–6: Love is not jealous or conceited or proud (v. 4 MSG). It doesn't force itself on others, isn't always "me first," doesn't fly off the handle, and doesn't keep score of the sins of others (v. 5 MSG). It doesn't revel when others grovel (v. 6 MSG). Ouch! How many of us are guilty of these, especially when it comes to the people we love most!

For example, verse 5 hits me especially hard. I can't begin to count how many times I have been in an argument with my husband, and to make my point, I'll bring up some record of his past wrong-doings toward me. Then he will follow suit, and before I know it, we've both drudged up painful memories and put ourselves in a bad place. Can anyone relate? Well, as we see in the scripture, this type of behavior is anti-love—it is the exact *opposite* of love, and we have to work daily toward not exhibiting such behavior.

It takes practice and determination to not act selfishly, behave proudly, or become easily irritated. From my encounters with other Christians, I've observed that the first and last parts of the passage are particularly difficult for them. Take the first part, "love doesn't force itself on others"—this makes me consider all the times I've seen many well-intentioned believers try to "shove" the Word of God "down peoples' throats." In this verse we see that this is NOT love. We should not force ourselves (or our beliefs) on others when they object to us doing so.

Consider this: God did not make us robots; rather He gave us the free will to choose whether or not to accept Jesus as our Savior. So how much more ought we to respect the free will of others the same way that God does! Our *best* way to witness to someone is how *we live* our lives and by how we show love. If you want to win souls to Christ, walk in love at all times, and that will draw others *to you*, and cause them to ask you how you are able to do it.

The last part of the passage says that love doesn't rejoice when someone else is down, but have you ever heard someone say something like, "Good! She got what she deserved!"?

> *Our best way to witness to someone is how we live our lives and by how we show love.*

Well, this also is not love. Christians tend to be some of the most judgmental people that exist, but many other scriptures (which we will visit later) discuss the folly and detriment that will come to *them* for judging others.

Let us now examine what love *is*, and how to show it. To find the answers we will revisit 1 Corinthians, and also look at 1 John. 1 Corinthians 13:4–8 (GNT) says that love "is patient and kind" (v. 4), "is happy with the truth" (v. 6), and "is eternal" (v. 8). *The Message* version in verse 8 also says that love "puts up with anything, trusts God always, always looks for the best, never looks back, but keeps going to the end."

Reading these definitions, it seems that meeting the biblical standard for achieving a truly loving spirit is impossible to live up to. I believe this is on purpose, so that we will always and forever strive to become *better at loving* others. Romans 13:8 (MSG) says "don't run up debts, except for the huge debt of love you owe each other." This means that we should strive to pay all of our debts except for the debt of love, for love can never be paid in full. Rather, we should always be working on making our love perfect, and giving and loving more and more all the time.

Furthermore, 1 John 4:20–21 (MSG) says, "If anyone boasts, 'I love God,' and goes right on hating his brother or sister, thinking nothing of it, he is a liar. If he won't love the person he can see, how can he love the God he can't see? *The command we have from*

Christ is blunt. Loving God includes loving people. You've got to love both." [Emphasis added.] Not only do we need to be patient, kind, honest, optimistic, and eternal in our love to our brother and sister, but in Matthew, we see that we also have to be this way with our enemies! Matthew 5:44 (MSG) says, "I'm telling you to love your enemies. Let them bring out the best in you, not the worst. When someone gives you a hard time, respond with the energies of prayer ...." Now *that* is the hard part, and one of the marks of a spiritually mature Christian. Luke 6:29–38 says:

> *If someone slaps you in the face, stand there and take it. If someone grabs your shirt, giftwrap your best coat and make a present of it. If someone takes unfair advantage of you, use the occasion to practice the servant life. No more tit-for-tat stuff. Live generously.*

> *Here is a simple rule of thumb for behavior: Ask yourself what you want people to do for you; then grab the initiative and do it for them! If you only love the lovable, do you except a pat on the back? Run-of-the-mill sinners do that. If you only help those who help you, do you expect a medal? Garden-variety sinners do that. If you only give for what you hope to get out if it, do you think*

that's charity? The stingiest of pawnbrokers does that.

I tell you, love your enemies. Help and give without expecting a return. You'll never—I promise—regret it. Live out this God-created identity the way our Father lives toward us, generously and graciously, even when we're at our worst. Our Father is kind; you be kind.

Don't pick on people, jump on their failures, and criticize their faults—unless, of course, you want the same treatment. Don't condemn those who are down; that hardness can boomerang. Be easy on people; you'll find life a lot easier. Give away your life; you'll find life given back, but not merely given back—given back with bonus and blessing. Giving, not getting, is the way. Generosity begets generosity. (MSG)

It is easy to love your fan club, but much more difficult to love your critics; however, this is exactly what Christians are commanded to do. We are to love everyone, even those we don't like, and in doing this, we can be a great example of God's love. The passage above gives descriptive examples of how to show love, and also gives us a glimpse into the rewards we will reap for demonstrating God's love to our enemies (or the penalties we will incur for not demonstrating God's love).

I encourage you today to think of some ways you can show God's love to others, especially those who don't deserve it. For example, when someone cuts me off in traffic, is rude to me, or provides me poor customer service, rather than "giving them a piece of my mind," I have resolved to just smile and say, "God bless you." I've also resolved to serve people in ways that are meaningful to them, give to the poor, and encourage those who are down. These are some ways I can love others and also honor God (we will talk more about honoring God later). Another passage that gives examples of how to be loving Christians can be found in Romans 12:6–21:

> *Let's just go ahead and be what we were made to be, without enviously or pridefully comparing ourselves with each other, or trying to be something we aren't.*
>
> *If you preach, just preach God's Message, nothing else; if you help, just help, don't take over; if you teach, stick to your teaching; if you give encouraging guidance, be careful that you don't get bossy; if you're put in charge, don't manipulate; if you're called to*

give aid to people in distress, keep your eyes open and be quick to respond; if you work with the disadvantaged, don't let yourself get irritated with them or depressed by them. Keep a smile on your face.

Love from the center of who you are; don't fake it. Run for dear life from evil; hold on for dear life to good. Be good friends who love deeply; practice playing second fiddle.

Don't burn out; keep yourselves fueled and aflame. Be alert servants of the Master, cheerfully expectant. Don't quit in hard times; pray all the harder. Help needy Christians; be inventive in hospitality.

Bless your enemies; no cursing under your breath. Laugh with your happy friends when they're happy; share tears when they're down. Get along with each other; don't be stuck-up. Make friends with nobodies; don't be the great somebody.

Don't hit back; discover beauty in everyone. If you've got it in you, get along with everybody. Don't insist on getting even; that's not for you to do. "I'll do the judging," says God. "I'll take care of it."

Our Scriptures tell us that if you see your enemy hungry, go buy that person lunch, or if he's thirsty, get him a drink. Your generosity will surprise him with goodness. Don't let evil get the best of you; get the best of evil by doing good. (MSG)

Love is EVERYTHING. It's the reason why we exist. It's the greatest commandment of all, and if we are not living a life of love, why should God give us one more breath to breathe? The importance of love is underscored in 1 Corinthians 13:1–3:

If I speak with human eloquence and angelic ecstasy but don't love, I'm nothing but the creaking of a rusty gate.

If I speak God's Word with power, revealing all his mysteries and making everything plain as day, and if I have faith that says to a mountain, "Jump," and it jumps, but I don't love, I'm nothing.

If I give everything I own to the poor and even go to the stake to be burned as a martyr, but I don't love, I've gotten nowhere. So, no matter what I say, what I believe, and what I do, I'm bankrupt without love. (MSG)

Without love, we cannot *know* Christ, we definitely cannot be *like* Christ, and we *certainly* can't please Christ. *Without love, we are NOTHING.*

Christ-Like Character

Fruits of the Spirit

One of the other questions I wanted to address is "what character traits should Christians possess?" I think that looking at the scripture passages regarding the fruit of the Spirit and the beatitudes give insight into what "real" believers really look like, and how they act.

Maybe you have seen T-shirts or other Christian paraphernalia that say, "Got Fruit?" These come from the teachings in the Bible regarding how it should be evident outwardly that we have the heart and mind of Christ within. When we (the branches) are attached to

Jesus (the vine), we should take on His characteristics. The book of John gives us this great analogy:

> I am the real vine, and my Father is the gardener. He breaks off every branch in me that does not bear fruit, and he prunes every branch that does bear fruit, so that it will be clean and bear more fruit. You have been made clean already by the teaching I have given you. Remain united to me, and I will remain united to you. A branch cannot bear fruit unless you remain in me.
>
> I am the vine, and you are the branches. Those who remain in me, and I in them, will bear much fruit; for you can do nothing without me. Those who do not remain in me are thrown out like a branch and dry up; such branches are gathered up and thrown into the fire, where they are burned. If you remain in me and my words remain in you, then you will ask for anything you wish, and you shall have it. My Father's glory is shown by your bearing much fruit; and in this way you become his disciples.
>
> —John 15:1–8 (GNT)

Just as healthy plants that are watered and properly cared for produce fruit, so should we, when fed the Word of God and through relationship with Christ, live fruitful and victorious lives. Matthew 12:33 (MSG) says, "If you grow a healthy tree, you'll pick healthy fruit. If you grow a diseased tree, you'll pick worm-eaten fruit. The fruit tells you about the tree." So others, without even knowing that we are Christians, should be able to tell that we are different by the character traits that our fruit produces, and by how God has blessed us.

Paul describes the "fruit of the Spirit" in the New Testament. Galatians 5:22–23 (GNT) says the fruit of the Spirit are "love, joy, peace, patience, kindness, goodness, faithfulness, humility, and self-control." It seems quite fitting that the first "fruit" mentioned is love. Since we have covered love quite extensively already, we will proceed with briefly discussing the other eight fruit.

The dictionary describes *joy* as "a feeling of great pleasure and happiness," but this is not how the Bible describes it. When I was a child, my dad explained joy to me this way: "joy is like happiness, but it is from within, and unlike happiness, it is not dependent on external circumstances." No matter what happens in the world, how bad the day is, how well or poor you are doing financially, etc., you can still have JOY in your heart. This is why the Bible says in Nehemiah 8:10 (NLT) that "the joy of the Lord is your strength." One way it is easy to spot a Christian is that even in difficult times, they are still radiating joy from within.

It is also important to know that no one can TAKE our joy—we have to GIVE it away. John 16:22 (MSG) says, "You'll be full of joy, and it will be a joy no one can rob from you." There will always be opportunities throughout the day for us to be sad, frustrated, and irritable, but John 14:27 says that the Lord has given us the power to stay calm in the time of adversity. So when someone is rude to you, look at it as an opportunity to stay calm, let Christ shine through you, and retain your joy!

Peace is defined as "freedom from disturbance; quiet and tranquility." Even more so, we see in the Bible that it is a state of contentment, assurance, and harmony (within and between individuals). It is a rest for our minds and souls that only God can give us. John 14:27 (GNT) says "Peace is what I leave with you; it is my own peace that I give you. I do not give it as the world does. Do not be worried and upset; do not be afraid." Jesus assures us over and over again that we can rest in Him, and that we should not be worried, anxious, or afraid because we can find peace in His presence, and because He will always provide for us, giving us exactly what we need.

Matthew 11:28 (GNT) says, "Come to me, all of you who are tired from carrying heavy loads, and I will give you rest." Philippians 4:6–7 (GNT) says, "Don't worry about anything, but in all your prayers ask God for what you need, always asking him with a thankful heart. And God's peace, which is far beyond human understanding, will keep your hearts and minds safe in union with Christ Jesus." When we are at peace, this shows God that we trust Him.

Furthermore, we are to demonstrate peace *outwardly*, by being peaceable toward one another. Romans 14:17–19 (GNT) says, "For God's Kingdom is not a matter of eating and drinking, but of the righteousness, peace, and joy, which the Holy Spirit gives. And when you serve Christ in this way, you please God and are approved by others. So then, we must always aim at those things that bring peace and that help strengthen one another."

Second Corinthians 13:11–12 (GNT) says, "And now, my friends, good-bye! Strive for perfection; listen to my appeals; agree with one another; live in peace. And the God of love and peace will be with you. Greet one another with the kiss of peace." Mark 9:50 (GNT) says, "Salt is good; but if it loses its saltiness, how can you make it salty again? Have the salt of friendship among yourselves, and live in peace with one another." Romans 12:18 (GNT) says "Do everything possible on your part to live in peace with everybody." There are many other verses about peace, both internal and external, but I think you get the picture. Just as God gives us peace, we should also strive to live peaceably.

Patience, also called long-suffering in the Bible, is defined as the "capacity to accept or tolerate delay, trouble, or suffering without getting angry or upset." It is the ability to endure difficult situations without getting angry. It is the capacity to be "slow to speak and quick to listen." This one is definitely a toughie! But if we want to be real Christians, others should see the fruit of patience in our lives. We shouldn't get upset and flick someone off in traffic when we get cut off. Rather, in such difficult situations we should remain "calm *and* cool *and* steady" (2 Timothy 4:5, Amplified), because when we don't, not only are we *not* demonstrating patience, but we are also giving away our joy and preventing God from blessing us!

Kindness and **goodness** go hand and hand—it is nearly impossible to have one without the other. Kindness is a sweet and friendly disposition, or the act or state of being friendly and benevolent. Goodness is the selfless desire to be generous to others. Usually when someone is genuinely doing something good, it is out of the kindness of their hearts. Out of a kind heart, good actions follow. Much like how faith is the evidence of things we can't see (Hebrews 11:1), goodness is the evidence of a kind heart.

Ephesians 4:32 (NLT) says, "Be kind to each other, tenderhearted, forgiving one another, just as God through Christ has forgiven you." Proverbs 3:3–4 says, "Never let loyalty and kindness leave you! Tie them around your neck as a reminder. Write them deep within your heart. Then you will find favor with both God and people, and you will earn a good reputation" (NLT). Here we see that not only are we commanded to be kind, but we see the amazing rewards that come as a result of being kind.

In the Bible, goodness is more consistent with generous and charitable *behavior* towards others. We frequently see in the Bible that God is good, and that all good things come from Him, and that Jesus's life was about doing good works. 1 Chronicles 16:34 (NLT) says, "Give thanks to the Lord, for He is good! His faithful love endures forever." James 1:17 (NLT) says, "Whatever is good and perfect comes down to us from God our Father, who created all the lights in the heavens." And Acts 10:38 (NLT) says, "Then Jesus went around doing good and healing all who were oppressed by the devil, for God was with Him."

We then, should also be concerned with doing good works, just as Christ did. Not only is this Christ-like behavior, but it also (like many of the other behaviors we've seen thus far) comes with rewards! Galatians 6:9–10 (NLT) says, "So let's not get tired of doing what is good. At just the right time we will reap a harvest of blessing if we don't give up. Therefore, whenever we have the opportunity, we should do good to everyone—especially to those in the family of faith." Proverbs 11:25 (NLT) says, "The generous will prosper; those who refresh others will themselves be refreshed."

Faithfulness is being trustworthy and reliable. A faithful person is deeply devoted to God, loyal to friends, and dependable to carry out any task that is asked. Jesus gives us insight into faithfulness with the parable of the servants found in Matthew 25:14–30, and also in Luke 12:42–48. In these passages we see that we are expected to be good stewards over what God has blessed us with (money, our children, etc.).

Revelation 2:10 (GNT) says, "The Devil will put you to the test .... Be faithful to me, even if it means death, and I will give your life as your prize of victory." In other words, act on what you say that you believe, and trust God to reward you for being faithful. We can also reexamine Proverbs 3:3, as it fits here as well (i.e., loyalty=faithfulness). We should also be faithful to God and labor for Him, and when we do these things, as we've seen many times before, we will be rewarded.

The proof of this is in Colossians 3:23–24 (GNT): "Whatever you do, work at it with all your heart, as though you were working for the Lord and not for people. Remember that the Lord will give you as a reward what He has kept for His people. For Christ is the real Master you serve."

In the scriptures we see that gentleness is also referred to as meekness or **humility**. It is a calm, humble, and non-threatening demeanor that is not to be confused with weakness. I've heard it described by many a preacher as "strength under control" and a "submissive spirit unto God." Jesus describes Himself as gentle and humble in heart in Matthew 11:28–30. Titus 3:1–2 (GNT) speaks of proper Christian conduct in regards to kindness, goodness, and gentleness: "Remind your people to submit to rulers and authorities, to obey them, and to be ready to do good in every way. Tell them not to speak evil of anyone, but to be peaceful and friendly, and always to show a gentle attitude toward everyone."

There are many real-world benefits to humility and gentleness, for example in Proverbs 15:1 (MSG), we see that "a gentle response defuses anger, but a sharp tongue kindles a temper-fire." We also see in Isaiah 29:19 and Psalm 147:6 some of the promises directed toward humble people—God promises to raise them up, bless them, and give them true happiness.

Self-control is the ability to successfully manage one's own impulses, actions, emotions, and desires;

and hold them accountable to God's Word. It is living rightly before God, and not selfishly according to one's own will. Jesus gave us the ultimate example of what it means to live our lives for God and not ourselves. We see in Luke 22:41–42 and 1 Peter 2:23 that people accused, threatened, ridiculed, and eventually crucified Him, but He did not retaliate. He could have easily destroyed everyone, but rather He prayed "Father ... not my will, but yours be done."

So the Bible also urges us to live our lives under (God's) control. There are several proverbs stressing the importance of self-control. Proverbs 16:32 (MSG) says, "Moderation is better than muscle, self-control better than political power" and chapter 25 verse 28 says, "A person without self-control is like a house with its doors and windows knocked out" (MSG). Self-control is also a theme throughout Titus chapter 2 (where Paul is encouraging the teaching of self-control in the church). We should be disciplined in *every* area of our lives, including but not limited to our food/alcohol consumption, our tempers, our finances, and in our sexual desires (outside of marriage).

In conclusion, the Bible gives us great understanding regarding the character traits or "fruit" we should possess. And not only does living lives full of the evidence of our "fruit" make us more "Christ-like," as we have seen time and again, it also allows us to reap many benefits and rewards. So as I asked in the beginning of this discussion, "Got Fruit?"

The Beatitudes

The beatitudes are teachings of Jesus that give us further insight into righteous living, and how to please God and find true happiness. They are found in Matthew 5:3–12 (GNT):

> *Happy are those who know they are spiritually poor; the Kingdom of heaven belongs to them!*
>
> *Happy are those who mourn; God will comfort them!*
>
> *Happy are those who are humble; they will receive what God has promised!*
>
> *Happy are those whose greatest desire is to do what God requires; God will satisfy them fully!*

Happy are those who are merciful to others; God will be merciful to them!

Happy are the pure in heart; they will see God!

Happy are those who work for peace; God will call them His children!

Happy are those who are persecuted because they do what God requires; the Kingdom of heaven belongs to them!

Happy are you when people insult you and persecute you and tell all kinds of evil lies against you because you are my followers. Be happy and glad, for a great reward is kept for you in heaven. This is how the prophets who lived before you were persecuted.

(* Of note, in many translations, the word "happy" is substituted with "blessed.")

There has been much written about the beatitudes, and every one of these proverbs is worthy of deep study and reflection, but essentially these are what it means to be a true disciple of Christ. We should be spiritually poor, meaning that we should recognize that we *need* Jesus. When Jesus spoke of those "who mourn," He spoke of those who have a repentant heart and desire to be forgiven for their sins. As we have discussed, we should be meek and submissive to doing things God's way. We should desire to be righteous, or like Christ, and to also forgive and be generous towards others, just as we want God to continue to show us forgiveness, mercy, kindness, and generosity. We should also be pure and holy, be peaceable, and live for God unashamedly, even in the midst of ridicule or persecution. Not only does being a disciple of Christ carry rewards here on earth, but living in this way also helps us to "store up treasure in heaven."

Faith

Another prerequisite to pleasing God is having faith. The Bible defines faith as "the substance of things hoped for, and the evidence of things not seen." Hebrews chapter 11 describes many of the great people of faith in the Bible, and also states that, "It's impossible to please God apart from faith" (v. 6). Having faith in God requires us to believe both of these: that He exists, and that He cares enough to respond to those who seek Him (v. 7). It requires us to act on what God has told us, rather than what we see or what others tell us.

For example, God instructed Noah to build an ark so that he and his family would survive the flood. Noah built this large ship in the middle of dry land, having never even seen rain before, because of his faith in God (read Genesis chapters 6 and 7). As a result of his faith and obedience, his family was saved. His faith was all the evidence he needed to initiate the erection of the great ark—he didn't actually have to physically see the storm coming before he got started (and had he waited, it would have been too late). God gives us many promises in the Bible, and if we agree with Him, and live by faith, we can be so victorious!

Here is a practical, modern-day example: I once heard a story about a mother whose young son was running with the wrong crowd, and started using drugs, and joined a gang. Everyone else said that this young man was going to end up in prison or dead before he was sixteen. His mother, however, didn't agree with the naysayers, but with God. She quoted God's promises that her son would be "mighty in the land" and "blessed" (Psalm 112:2) and that as for she and her house, "they would serve the Lord" (Joshua

24:15). Even though she couldn't yet see her child turning around, her faith was the evidence that he had done so. She decided to agree with God rather than what she saw, or what others were saying. The result was that her son did change his life, and eventually ended up becoming the pastor of a church! There are many other examples to read about in Hebrews 11, but the take home point is that we can't please God, or live our best lives, without having faith.

A Christian's Obligations

Jesus taught much about what He expects of us as Christians in the book of Matthew, and other writers of the Bible also exhort us regarding how we should live as well. We will discuss our moral obligations one by one, in no particular order.

Love God, Love People

We have already extensively researched love, and as we have mentioned previously, Jesus said in Mark 12 that the most important commandment is to first love God (which includes having faith in Him, obeying

Him, and walking in right relationship with Him), and then to love others (He also says this in Matthew 22:37–40). We have also discussed how this includes even loving our enemies (Matthew 5:43–48 and Luke 6:27–36). This theme is repeated many times throughout the Bible.

Loving God means obeying His commandments, and worshipping Him, and honoring Him with our best praise. Proverbs 19:16 (GNT) says, "keep God's laws and you will live longer; if you ignore them, you will die," and John 14:15 (GNT) says simply, "if you love me, you will obey my commandments." In *The Message* translation of Matthew 7:21, Jesus says, "Knowing the correct password—saying 'Master, Master,' for instance—isn't going to get you anywhere with me. What is required is serious obedience—doing what my Father wills." And Matthew 4:10 (GNT) says, "Worship the Lord your God and serve only Him!"

Jesus outlines many criteria for how we should live, but in particular, it is my understanding that His "laws" refer to the Ten Commandments, which were given to Moses in Exodus 20:1–17. Briefly these say we: should not worship any false god(s), make or worship any images/idols, or use God's name irreverently, should observe the Sabbath day to keep it holy, honor your parents, and should not murder, commit adultery, steal, lie, or covet anything that belongs to your neighbor. We have already seen many scriptures regarding how we should love people, but a few more verses concerning loving others include 1 John 4:7–8, John 13:34–35, Galatians 5:13–14, and James 2:16. As we will continue to see, how much we love God is also indicated by how much we love others, and how consistently we live out our daily lives in ways that honor and please Him.

Live Righteously

The Bible instructs us in 1 Peter 1:14–16 that we should not do the same things worldly and unsaved people do, rather *we should be different*, and holy. It says, "Don't lazily slip back into those old grooves of evil, doing just what you feel like doing. You didn't know any better then; you do now. As obedient children, let yourselves be pulled into a way of life shaped by God's life, a life energetic and blazing with holiness. God said, 'I am holy; you be holy' " (MSG). Being holy is being entirely dedicated and devoted to

God, both inwardly and outwardly. It suggests not just moral purity (sexual purity, financial honesty, altruistic behavior, etc.), but also a right relationship with God (privately and publicly).

Everyone we know should know that we are Christians by the right way we live our lives. Matthew 5:14–16 (MSG) says, "Here's another way to put it: you're here to be light, bringing out the God-colors in the world. God is not a secret to be kept. We're going public with this, as public as a city on a hill. If I make you light-bearers, you don't think I'm going to hide you under a bucket, do you? I'm putting you on a light stand. Now that I've put you there on a hilltop, on a light stand—shine! Keep open house; be generous with your lives. By opening up to others, you'll prompt people to open up with God, this generous Father in heaven."

Being holy is being entirely dedicated and devoted to God, both inwardly and outwardly.

The New Living Translation of Romans 12:1–2 says, "And so, dear brothers and sisters, I plead with you to give your bodies to God because of all He has done for you. Let them be a living and holy sacrifice—the kind He will find acceptable. This is truly the way to worship Him. Don't copy the behavior and customs of this world, but let God transform you into a new person by changing the way you think. Then you will learn to know God's will for you, which is good and pleasing and perfect."

Paul makes it even more plain in 1 Corinthians 9:25–27 when he says, "all athletes train hard. They do it for a gold medal that tarnishes and fades. You're after one that's gold eternally. I don't know about you, but I'm running hard for the finish line. I'm giving it everything I've got. No sloppy living for me! I'm staying alert and in top condition. I'm not going to get caught napping, telling everyone else all about it and then missing out myself" (MSG). We should live in a way that is holy, dedicating our lives and everything we do to Christ; and we should not be ashamed of our faith, but rather be witnesses to God's matchless love and grace.

Spread the "Good News"

Jesus speaks in the Bible of us being "fishers of men," meaning being evangelists and winning souls to Christ. Because God has been so good to us, we should WANT to tell others of His goodness, power, grace, and love when we have the opportunity to do so. We should especially witness to people that we love. My dad always told me that it may initially be awkward, but isn't the eventual destination of their souls (being in heaven rather than hell) worth it? In Matthew 28:19–20, Jesus said, "Therefore, go and make disciples of all the nations, baptizing them in the name of the Father and the Son and the Holy Spirit. Teach these new disciples to obey all the commands I have given you. And be sure of this: I am with you always, even to the end of the age" (NLT).

He also says this in Mark 16:15–16, "Go throughout the whole world and preach the gospel to all people. Whoever believes and is baptized will be saved; whoever does not believe will be condemned" (GNT). This does not mean shove the Word of God down people's throats, or preach to people that don't want to listen to you—Jesus did not do these things—

and neither should we (besides these are neither kind nor loving actions). The best way to witness to others is with your love and generous actions, and with your lifestyle; these will draw people to you, and give you the opportunity to tell of God's goodness.

Tithe

There are a great number of passages in the Bible about tithing. The tithe is the first tenth of your increase (income, gifts, etc.), and it belongs to God. Every time we receive an increase, we are to give the first ten percent back to God as our tithe at our place of worship (our home church).

Proverbs 3:9–10 (MSG) says, "Honor God with everything you own; give him the first and the best. Your barns will burst, your wine vats will brim over." Furthermore, Malachi 3:8–11 (MSG) says, "Begin by being honest. Do honest people rob God? But you rob me day after day. You ask, 'How have we robbed you?' The tithe and offering—that's how! And now you're under a curse—the whole lot of you—because you're robbing me. Bring your full tithe to the Temple treasury so there will be ample provisions in my

Temple. Test me in this and see if I don't open up heaven itself to you and pour out blessings beyond your wildest dreams. For my part, I will defend you against marauders; protect your wheat fields and vegetable gardens from plunderers."

We tithe to God as a way to thank Him for His provision, as a gesture of trust and praise, and as an exchange for His protection over the other ninety percent of our money; and when we do (in an attitude of thanksgiving, not begrudgingly, 2 Cor. 9:7), God will bless us even more!

Be Good Stewards

Being a good steward entails responsibly and wisely managing the resources that God entrusts us with. It most obviously relates to money, but also relates to our homes, cars, children, and all of "our" possessions. As we discussed above, as Christians, we dedicate ourselves completely to God. We understand that nothing, not even our own bodies or our own children belong to us, but to God. My dad always said that God has "loaned" us these things for an appointed time, and we are to do our best to care for them.

Jesus tells us a story about stewardship in Matthew 25:14–30. Essentially, a master gave three of his servants gold to be stewards over while he was away. When he returned, two of the servants made good investments, and doubled the money while he was gone, and the master rejoiced with them, and gave them more money to watch over. However, the third servant just buried the master's money in the ground. When the master found out about this he was very angry, and not only did he take back all the money he gave him, but he also threw "him outside in the darkness" where he would "cry and gnash his teeth." We see here how important it is to responsibly manage what God gives us to look after. The lesson is that if we do well with what we are given, God will give us more; but if we are lazy, or don't manage well what we have, it will be taken away.

Let's make it plain: if you treat your junk car poorly, keep it filthy, and don't care for it, why do you think He would bless you with the car of your dreams? Luke 16:10 (NLT) says, "If you are faithful in little things, you will be faithful in large ones. But if you are dishonest in little things, you won't be honest with greater responsibilities. And if you are untrustworthy about worldly wealth, who will trust you with the true riches of heaven? And if you are not faithful with other people's things, why should you be trusted with things of your own?"

So being a good steward involves many things, not limited to providing for your household, relatives, and giving to the poor (1 Timothy 5:8, Leviticus 19:9–10, and Proverbs 11:24), investing wisely (Matthew 25:14–30), training your kids in Gods ways (Proverbs 22:6), and respecting/wisely managing all of the other resources God has already blessed you with (Luke 16:10).

Forgive

Christ teaches us throughout the Bible that it is important to forgive one another. He showed us grace and mercy by forgiving us our sins, even though we did not deserve it; so we also, in an effort to be like Christ, should forgive others, even when we feel they don't deserve it. Like most of Christ's commands, obedience in this regard grants us continual mercy, but failing to forgive results in penalties.

Matthew 6:14–15 (GNT) says, "If you forgive others the wrongs they have done to you, your Father in heaven will also forgive you. But if you do not forgive others, then your Father will not forgive the wrongs you have done." Mark 11:25 (GNT) says, "And when you stand and pray, forgive anything you may have against anyone, so that your Father in heaven will forgive the wrongs you have done." It is a scary thing to think about Jesus not forgiving us; without His forgiveness we would end up in hell! Jesus tells us a story about forgiveness in Matthew 18:21–35:

> *At that point Peter got up the nerve to ask, "Master, how many times do I forgive a brother or sister who hurts me? Seven?"*
>
> *Jesus replied, "Seven! Hardly. Try seventy times seven.*
>
> *"The kingdom of God is like a king who decided to square accounts with his servants. As he got under way, one servant was brought before him who had run up a debt of a hundred thousand dollars. He couldn't pay up, so the king ordered the man, along with*

his wife, children, and goods, to be auctioned off at the slave market.

"The poor wretch threw himself at the king's feet and begged, 'Give me a chance and I'll pay it all back.' Touched by his plea, the king let him off, erasing the debt.

"The servant was no sooner out of the room when he came upon one of his fellow servants who owed him ten dollars. He seized him by the throat and demanded, 'Pay up. Now!'

"The poor wretch threw himself down and begged, 'Give me a chance and I'll pay it all back.' But he wouldn't do it. He had him arrested and put in jail until the debt was paid. When the other servants saw this going on, they were outraged and brought a detailed report to the king.

"The king summoned the man and said, 'You evil servant! I forgave your entire debt when you begged me for mercy. Shouldn't you be compelled to be merciful to your fellow servant who asked for mercy?' The king was furious and put the screws to the man until he paid back his entire debt. And that's exactly what my Father in heaven is going to do to each one of you who doesn't forgive

unconditionally anyone who asks for mercy."
(MSG)

Do Good

"Doing good" is a very important premise in the Bible. Not only do we see it mentioned as a fruit of the Spirit and in the beatitudes (as previously discussed), but we also see it mentioned in several other passages. So we, in our never-ending quest to be Christ-like, should go about doing good deeds, the same way that Jesus did. Recall what Acts 10:38 (GNT) says about Jesus: "He went everywhere, doing good and healing all who were under the power of the Devil, for God was with Him."

In fact, the gospels (Matthew, Mark, Luke, and John) are filled with examples of how Jesus went about doing good works, helping, and healing people. In Matthew 8, He healed a leper. In Matthew 9, He healed a paralyzed man, a bleeding woman, a girl, and the blind and mute. In Matthew 15, He cast out demons, healed many more people, and fed over four thousand people! Please read the aforementioned four gospels to find many more examples.

We are not only responsible for our own families, but also for helping others in need, just as Jesus did. It is easy (and our job) to give good things to our children, but how do we stack up when it comes to others? The poor? The hopeless? Galatians 6:7–10 (MSG) says, "Don't be misled: No one makes a fool of God. What a person plants, he will harvest. The person who plants selfishness, ignoring the needs of others—ignoring God!—harvests a crop of weeds. All he'll have to show for his life is weeds! But the one who plants in response to God, letting God's Spirit do the growth work in him, harvests a crop of real life, eternal life. So let's not allow ourselves to get fatigued doing good. At the right time we will harvest a good crop if we don't give up, or quit. Right now, therefore, every time we get the chance, let us work for the benefit of all, starting with the people closest to us in the community of faith."

Hebrews 10:24 (GNT) says, "Let us be concerned for one another, to help one another to show love and to do good." There are many ways to "do good": for instance mentoring, volunteering at church or with a community charity, ministering God's love through mission trips, giving of our time *and money,* etcetera;

but the key is that we be consistent, and perform these acts out of love, and not for recognition or appearances. (As an aside—Christians can be really good at praying for someone with a need, but often times are not good at actually *helping* them. If someone is hungry, don't just pray for them, but also buy them a meal, see James 2:16).

In fact, Jesus says in Matthew 6:1–4 (GNT), "Make certain you do not perform your religious duties in public so that people will see what you do. If you do these things publicly, you will not have any reward from your Father in heaven. So when you give something to a needy person, do not make a big show of it, as the hypocrites do in the houses of worship and on the streets. They do it so that people will praise them. I assure you, they have already been paid in full. But when you help a needy person, do it in such a way that even your closest friend will not know about it. Then it will be a private matter. And your Father, who sees what you do in private, will reward you."

We should constantly be looking for ways to be good to people. The Bible says in Galatians 6:10 that we should never miss an opportunity to bless people. In fact, we were created to give. Luke 6:38 says that

"Giving, not getting is the way. Generosity begets generosity." God takes notice of even the smallest acts of kindness (buying someone a cup of coffee, letting someone in front of you in traffic), and He will always pay us back. When you bless others, God will bless you. The way to truly have an enriched life filled with joy is to not focus on what we can get, but what we can give.

Other Things

In the books of Matthew and others, Jesus also mentions several other things we should be doing. He speaks much about serving one another, and how the greatest of us is willing to be the least (Mark 10:44, 1 John 3:16). He also teaches us about prayer and how to do it (see the Lord's Prayer, Matthew 6), and about fasting, and why and how to do it (also Matthew 6). There are many lessons to be learned, many of which I'm sure I still need to learn, and can only come from thoroughly exploring God's Word.

Don't Do These Things

When trying to decipher how to walk with Christ, sometimes it is just as beneficial to know what *not* to do as it is to know what *to* do. It is obvious that we should not break any of the Ten Commandments, but the following are some other things that the Bible tells us we should avoid so as not to be hypocrites (which damages our credibility as Christians, and repels others away from us and from wanting to be Christians). I'm going to warn you now, some of these may be hard pills to swallow, and may even be quite controversial (to some "religious" folk), but these admonitions come straight from the Bible, with references included.

Don't Judge

This is a hard one for Christians! We really have to stop being so critical of other people, especially when we know that we too are sinners saved only by the grace of Almighty God. It is very easy to condemn those whose sins are public knowledge, but *every one* of us has sinned, and most of us sin in one way or another every day—the only difference being that most of the time no one else *knows* our sins. Matthew 7:1–5 (MSG) says this:

> *Don't pick on people, jump on their failures, criticize their faults—unless, of course, you want the same treatment. That critical spirit has a way of boomeranging. It's easy to see a smudge on your neighbor's face and be oblivious to the ugly sneer on your own. Do you have the nerve to say, "Let me wash your face for you," when your own face is distorted by contempt? It's this whole traveling road-show mentality all over again, playing a holier-than-thou part*

instead of just living your part. Wipe that ugly sneer off your own face, and you might be fit to offer a washcloth to your neighbor.

When I read this verse, for some reason I think of the "Christians" who stand outside of abortion clinics jeering at the women going inside, judging them, and telling them how sinful they are. Get over yourselves! How would you feel if someone stood outside your house or place of business holding up signs about all the things you do wrong? Again, the only difference is that you keep your dirt hidden. If you have enough time to sit outside and condemn people that you don't even know (and worse, don't even know their situation), then you are not "living your part" or leading a very useful life.

Titus 3:14 (GNT) says, "Our people must learn to spend their time doing good, in order to provide for real needs; they should not live useless lives." Here we see leading a useful life is equated to providing for the *real* needs of others. Instead of hurling insults at women entering abortion clinics and trying to show them grotesque images to prove to them that they are bad people deserving of shame and condemnation, do something productive with your lives—maybe start a nonprofit that focuses on showing these women love, and helping them to cope and heal, while sharing the Good News of God's goodness and mercy towards us all. Go do something GOOD and useful for someone else.

Remember, "It wasn't so long ago that we ourselves were stupid and stubborn, dupes of sin, ordered every which way by our glands, going around with a chip on our shoulder, hated and hating back. But when God, our kind and loving Savior God, stepped in, He saved us from all that. It was all His doing; we had nothing to do with it. He gave us a good bath, and we came out of it new people, washed inside and out by the Holy Spirit. Our Savior Jesus poured out new life so generously" (Titus 3:3–6, MSG). It would also do us good to remember our first and most important job is to *love* people unconditionally.

Furthermore God LOVES imperfect people (this is comforting, because while many Christians live to give a perfect *performance*, the reality is that we are all imperfect people). There is actually evidence in the Bible that God *prefers* imperfect people—those who have a "cold heart" to Him and who live to gratify themselves and care nothing for Him—to Christians who continue to sin/live unrighteously. Revelation 3:15–16 (NLT) says, "I know all the things you do, that you are neither hot nor cold. I wish that you were one or the other! But since you are like lukewarm water, neither hot nor cold, I will spit you out of my mouth!" In other words, God would rather you be completely sinful, because at least then you wouldn't be a hypocrite.

Throughout the Bible God is referred to as the God of "Abraham, Isaac, and Jacob." While Abraham and Isaac were great men of faith, Jacob was a liar and a thief, yet God loved him just as much. So too does he love the "outsiders" that Christians often condemn ... He died for them. We should all be more like Him, and rather than judge/shame/condemn those who are living in sin, we should love, accept, and encourage them so that we can offer physical proof of God's love. After all, true love is *action* ... how *good* you are to people is a more clear and effective message than the most elegant sermon.

Do any of you remember the Casey Anthony trial? It was a really big deal here in Florida, and it is still newsworthy from time to time. At any rate, Casey is a young mother who was accused of killing her little girl. She was (and probably still is, even though she was acquitted) the most hated woman in Florida. The revelation God gave me regarding my attitude toward her is what inspired me to write this book.

During the height of the trial, you couldn't go a day without hearing about how terrible a woman she was and how she should rot in jail. And I will be the first to admit, I was right there with them. I remember thinking, "it's a good thing I'm not God, I know where I'd send her" (which is the same thing I thought about the Penn State coaches, the Catholic priests, and countless other "evil" people). But then God gave me a revelation. John 3:16–17 (GNT) says, "For God loved the world so much that He gave His only Son, so that everyone who believes in Him may not die but have eternal life. For God did not send His Son into the world to be its judge, but to be its savior."

So the first point is that even *Jesus* didn't come to judge us, so how can we judge each other? Secondly, the scripture says *everyone* can have a chance at redemption (by believing in Christ)—and that includes murderers, rapists, adulterers, liars, and more. If Casey, or the Catholic priests, or any other "terrible" sinner repented and gave their lives to Christ, they would end up in heaven just like you (if you are saved).

Isaiah 53:4–6 (GNT) says, "But He endured the suffering that should have been ours, the pain that we should have borne. All the while we thought that His suffering was punishment sent by God. But because of our sins He was wounded, beaten because of the evil we did. We are healed by the

The point is that Jesus shed a lot of blood so that we could be saved from our sins.

punishment He suffered, made whole by the blows He received. All of us were like sheep that were lost, each of us going his own way. But the Lord made the punishment fall on Him, the punishment all of us deserved." (If you want a more graphic account of His death you can read more in Matthew 27, Luke 23, or John 19.)

The point is that Jesus shed a lot of blood so that we could be saved from our sins. It is not about Casey (or anyone) being so evil that they *deserve* punishment or *don't deserve* forgiveness; rather it is about God being so good and merciful that He *deserves* the opportunity to show each and every person love and mercy if they desire to accept it. He *deserves* that every single drop of His precious blood be put to good use—not a single drop should be wasted. So we then, should not judge or hate anyone, but rather attempt to share our faith with others in love. God did not create us to be spiritual referees or judges, but to build one another up, and be ambassadors of God's limitless love and mercy.

The NLT version of James 4:11–12 says, "Don't speak evil against each other dear brothers and sisters. If you criticize and judge each other, then you are criticizing and judging God's law. But your job is to obey the law, not to judge whether it applies to you. God alone, who gave the law, is the Judge. He alone has the power to save or to destroy. So what right do you have to judge your neighbor?"

Of course, this is not to say that people who commit crimes against others shouldn't be punished if they break the law (the Bible is clear that everyone should obey the laws of their own governments, Titus 3:1). This is also not to say that we should be okay with sin, because we shouldn't. It is perfectly fine to take a strong stance against evil and sin, but we are to love the *sinner*. For example, it is fine to not approve of homosexuality (a sin per the Bible, see Romans 1:27), but you are still supposed to love homosexuals *and not judge them.* It is fine to not approve of abortion, but you are to show *love* to women who may have just had an abortion *and not judge them.* And not only that, but you should not proselytize—if you do not approve, then *you* should not participate in these activities. But it is not your business to tell everyone else (particularly those who are not Christians) what they are doing wrong. After all, our job is to demonstrate our love, and live our best lives ... how we live is our best witness. (We will examine this position through scripture in the next few paragraphs.)

According to the Bible, if you "hate" anyone (who you consider to be sinful), you are far worse than they are. 1 John 3:15 (MSG) says, "Everyone who hates a brother or sister is a murderer, and you know very well that eternal life and murder don't go together."

In my research, I've come across many people incorrectly interpreting the scriptures to make it seem like we are supposed to be pointing out the sins of unbelievers, but I can find no such passages. Furthermore, every passage about correcting, admonishing, or pointing out sin in someone else (in *love*, of course) that I know of, is speaking about *other believers/Christians*, or if someone has specifically committed a sin against you *personally*.

Matthew 18:15–18 (NLT) says, "If another believer sins against *you*, go privately and point out the offense. If the other person listens and confesses it, you have won that person back. But if you are unsuccessful, take one or two others with you and go back again, so that everything you say may be confirmed by two or three witnesses. If the person still refuses to listen, take your case to the church. Then if he or she won't accept the church's decision, treat that person as a pagan or a corrupt tax collector."

We also see examples of when we should call out (someone *in the church*) for sexual sin (1 Corinthians 5:1–7) or "any other sin," but we are to do it with a gentle and humble spirit (Galatians 6:1–2) so as to save their souls from hell (also James 5:19, Colossians 3:16).

Further evidence that we should only be pointing out the sins of other *Christians* (in love) is found in 1 Corinthians 5:9–13 (NLT, emphasis added): "When I wrote to you before, I told you not to associate with people who indulge in sexual sin. But I wasn't talking about unbelievers who indulge in sexual sin, or are greedy, or cheat people, or worship idols. You would have to leave this world to avoid people like that. I meant that you are not to associate with anyone who claims to be a believer yet indulges in sexual sin, or is greedy, or worships idols, or is abusive, or is a drunkard, or cheats people. Don't even eat with such people. *It isn't my responsibility to judge outsiders, but it certainly is your responsibility to judge those inside the church who are sinning.* God will judge those on the outside; but as the Scriptures say, 'You must remove the evil person from among you.'" *The Message* translation puts it even more bluntly: *"I'm not responsible for what the outsiders do, but don't we have some responsibility for those within our community of believers?* (v. 12) *God decides on the outsiders, but we need to decide when our brothers and sisters are out of line and, if necessary, clean house"* (v. 13, emphasis added).

The book of Proverbs also makes reference to only attempting to correct those who already have some wisdom or knowledge of God in chapter 9 verses 7–9 (MSG). Here it says, "If you reason with an arrogant cynic, you'll get slapped in the face; confront bad behavior and get a kick in the shins. So don't waste your time on a scoffer; all you'll get for your pains is abuse. But if you correct those who care about life, that's different—they'll love you for it! Save your breath for the wise—they'll be wiser for it; tell good people what you know—they'll profit from it."

As Christians we shouldn't go about gossiping, condemning, criticizing, or trying to get revenge. We shouldn't act holier-than-thou, and try to shove the Gospel down the throats of unbelievers. We shouldn't try to point out the sins of unbelievers. (How can we win souls this way? Don't you think we would do better to talk of God's grace and compassion?) 1 Thessalonians 4:11–12 (NLT) says, "Make it your goal to live a quiet life, *minding your own business* and working with your hands, just as we

> *Stop hating on the gays and the abortion clinics … and mind your own business.*

instructed you before. Then people who are not Christians will respect the way you live, and you will not need to depend on others." *The Message* says it this way, "stay calm; mind your own business; do your own job...." We should show everyone love, and when our fellow believers fall, we should gently and humbly correct them and help them back up. However, we should be God's representatives to the unbelievers, sharing our testimonies, speaking of His goodness, and then trusting God to work on their hearts as we witness to them with our love and our lifestyles.

Stop hating on the gays and the abortion clinics (among many other vilified things), and mind your own business.

I know this will earn a lot of criticism, but I would even go so far as to say we shouldn't be campaigning politically against gay rights. Yes, I believe homosexuality is a sin, but we are instructed to leave other people's sin up to God. God didn't make us robots that would follow His Word to the letter; rather He gave us the freedom of choice, to choose whether or not to serve Him. So how can we then, try to force others to do what *we* say is right? We can't legislate people into living biblically correct lives. And what would be the point of passing laws to make an unbeliever live a more Christ-like life? How would that benefit them? We know that just following the law doesn't get you into heaven. Anyone who doesn't accept Christ as their Lord and Savior will still be judged by God. This is a choice they have to make for themselves!

Furthermore, there is no distinction in the Bible between the gravity of the sin of homosexuality and any other sin (drunkenness, greed, adultery, stealing, being mean or abusive, being dishonest/treating people unfairly, and etcetera, see 1 Cor. 6:9–10) except blasphemy of the Holy Spirit (this is the one sin that can never be forgiven).

Proverbs also mentions the seven sins God hates the most, and homosexuality is not among these (see Proverbs 6:16–19). So if you are a Christian and are mean to your spouse, or steal reams of paper from work, or drink too much, or are greedy for money, or are an arrogant person, you are just the same in God's eyes as someone who practices homosexuality! If you are arrogant, a liar, or a murderer, you are worse than one who practices homosexuality.

How many times have you heard of a pastor who cheated on his wife, or a church member who has cursed someone out? Believers all have their own issues to keep in check, and need to remember to keep their own faces washed. I urge all believers who do any of the above things and who may think they are any "holier" than a homosexual to think again. The only difference between the two is that once we (believers) commit our lives to Christ, we are candidates to receive God's mercy and forgiveness, and the right to live eternally with Him in heaven (if *we* don't judge, and if *we* also forgive and show mercy to others).

So the next time the "gay rights" argument comes up, why not surprise everyone in the room by supporting it? Why should they *not* have the same rights? If you want to be against them, why not also campaign for a law that prevents unwed women or teenagers from having children? We've all seen shows like *Teen Mom* on TV, and we know they don't live Christ-centered lives, right? When put in this perspective, it becomes easy to see how silly it is to try to legislate our personal beliefs. Homosexuality should not be vilified and singled out as more outrageous and despicable than any other sin that people (including Christians) commit daily. If you want to make homosexuality an issue (which you shouldn't), then you should make *everything* an issue (which is unreasonable).

Now I am not saying that we should keep our salvation a secret; as I previously stated, we should be excited to tell others about God's goodness! It is fine for us to share God's Word with others, but we have to trust God to be the ultimate judge, and that He will give justice as He promises He will in His Word—for God is a God of love, but He is also a God of justice. In fact, Romans 12:19 (MSG) says, "Don't insist on getting even; that's not for you to do. 'I'll do the judging,' says God. 'I'll take care of it.'"

We can't force a sinner to love God or live for God, nor should we try to; God doesn't do this, so should we be arrogant enough to try? God works on people's hearts all the time—consider Paul. This great prophet wrote nearly two-thirds of the New Testament in the Bible, but before he became a Christian he was a murderer. He murdered Christians for a living! But God appeared to him one day, and Paul's life was changed forever when he decided to live for HIM! Don't you know that when all of the martyred saints that Paul (formerly known as Saul) was personally responsible for killing saw him in heaven they probably thought "what is HE doing here?" God has shown us that He can change even the most resistant of hearts; so after we minister about His goodness (not about how bad someone is sinning), we have to leave the heart-changing up to Him.

I also don't believe that just because you are a Christian you have to be a republican. After all, we are not voting for America's bishop, but for the President of the United States. Why should we care if the president agrees or disagrees with same sex marriage or abortion? What does that have to do with anything? People can sin against their own bodies all they want, that is not for us to try to correct or legislate. What they do is between them and God, and they will answer to Him ALONE one day.

As stated above, we should be careful when approaching moral issues in a political way. Those who don't keep God's commands do not have to answer to us, nor should we want them to, because our judgmental behavior prevents us from receiving mercy and grace from God, without which we would all be going to hell. So I would advise anyone who votes to vote based on the candidate who has ideas that would best ensure the success of this country.

Finally, to sum up regarding this judgment issue, I just want to leave you with some food for thought.

Christians, especially pastors in the pulpit here in Florida, were very quick to rush to judgment against Casey Anthony, but were equally quick to suppress any negative press about a pastor here who I will call "Timothy Zimmerman." Pastor Timothy was engaged in a notorious affair with a stripper, and died in a hotel room where a "powdery white substance" was found near his body. (We will address pastors specifically later on.) Shouldn't they have done just the opposite, according to the scriptures?

According to 1 Corinthians 5:1–7, Pastor Timothy should have been called out about his sexual sins, and according to 1 Corinthians 5:12–13, he should have been removed from the church (or at least from the leadership). It was the church's responsibility to correct him, not cover up for him, because he had a chance to be reeled-in, yet no one cared enough to do so; or at least it seems if they did care, it was only about the *idea* of him, and not his actual soul.

I even heard one pastor say to his congregation that they should not even look at or listen to any news reports about the late pastor because he was such a great man of God; encouraging us all to just pretend everything we had heard was not true. I was not in attendance at Pastor Timothy's funeral, but from all accounts, many excuses were made for his behavior, and much speculation was made that he was in heaven because of the many exploits he did in Christ's name. I do not claim to know the final resting spot of this man's soul, but I do know that Matthew 7:21–23 (MSG) says this, "Knowing the correct password— saying 'Master, Master,' for instance—isn't going to get you anywhere with me. What is required is serious obedience—doing what my Father wills. I can see it now—at the Final Judgment thousands strutting up to me and saying, 'Master, we preached the Message, we bashed the demons, our God-sponsored projects had everyone talking.' And do you know what I am going to say? 'You missed the boat. All you did was use me to make yourselves important. You don't impress me one bit. You're out of here.'"

Perhaps if someone would have been responsible for this man's soul rather than responsible for calling a publicist to save face, he might still be alive; and his testimony could have helped other men and women with the same struggles. The church has a lot of work to do. Stop offering your washcloth to other people before you wash your own face.

Divorce

There are many other things the Bible warns Christians against doing. I will attempt to list as many of them here as I can think of, but I'm sure there are many more. For one, we shouldn't get divorced. Mark 10:9, 11–12 (MSG) says, "Because God created this organic union of the two sexes, no one should desecrate His art by cutting them apart ... a man who divorces his wife so he can marry someone else commits adultery against her. And a woman who divorces her husband so she can marry someone else commits adultery."

This is not to say there is never a reason for a divorce. In fact, the Bible states that unfaithfulness (Matthew 19:9) and abuse (2 Timothy 3:1–5, Ephesians 5:11, Proverbs 22:24) are grounds for divorce; but it is not okay to divorce someone just because you have "grown apart" or feel like you don't love them anymore, or want to be with someone new. This being said, even if one does get a divorce, that is not the end, and contrary to what some pastors preach, this will not send you to hell. There is always forgiveness for true repentance, as God's mercy is unfailing (1 John 1:9, Proverbs 28:13, etc.).

Sexual Sin, Drunkenness

Christians should not commit sexual sins. The Bible addresses a variety of scenarios that qualify as such including the following: adultery (sex outside of your marriage), fornication (premarital sex), homosexuality (same gender sex), bestiality (sex with animals), and incest (sex with relatives). It is important to consider these scenarios, as during these contemporary times, many of these are now "the norm." However the Word of God is our standard, and regardless of what society deems to be tolerable or acceptable, we have to keep our behaviors subject to the authority of God's everlasting Word.

Please see these passages of scripture for further explanation and substantiation of the above: Exodus 20:14, Leviticus 18, Deuteronomy 5:18, 1 Corinthians 7:2, 2 Corinthians 12:21, Galatians 5:19, and Hebrews 13:4. In 1 Corinthians 10:8 it says, "We must not be sexually promiscuous."

The NLT version of Ephesians 5:3 says, "Let there be no sexual immorality, impurity, or greed among you. Such sins have no place among God's people." It also says in 1 Thessalonians 4:3–7, "God's will is for you to be holy, so stay away from all sexual sin. Then each of you will control his own body and live in holiness and honor—not in lustful passion like the pagans who do not know God and His ways. Never harm or cheat a Christian brother in the matter by violating his wife, for the Lord avenges all such sins, as we have solemnly warned you before. God has called us to live holy lives, not impure lives."

The NLT version of 1 Corinthians 6:9–10 says, "Don't you realize that those who do wrong will not inherit the Kingdom of God? Don't fool yourselves. Those who indulge in sexual sin, or who worship idols, or commit adultery, or are male prostitutes, or practice homosexuality, or are thieves, or greedy people, or drunkards, or are abusive, or cheat people—none of these will inherit the Kingdom of God." 1 Corinthians 6:12–20 has even more to say about keeping your body pure and holy.

Many Other Things

Galatians 5:19–21 (NLT) gives further instructions on things we shouldn't do if we want to go to heaven: "When you follow the desires of your sinful nature, the results are very clear: sexual immorality, impurity, lustful pleasures, idolatry, sorcery, hostility, quarreling, jealousy, outbursts of anger, selfish ambition, dissension, division, envy, drunkenness, wild parties, and other sins like these. Let me tell you again, as I have before, that anyone living that sort of life will not inherit the Kingdom of God."

Jesus also spoke about not making empty promises: "And don't say anything you don't mean ... You only make things worse when you lay down a smoke screen of pious talk, saying, 'I'll pray for you,' and never doing it, or saying, 'God be with you,' and not meaning it. You don't make your words true by embellishing them with religious lace. In making your speech sound more religious, it becomes less true. Just say 'yes' and 'no.' When you manipulate words to get your own way, you go wrong" (Matthew 5:33–37, MSG). In the same chapter, He also says we shouldn't be angry with one another, and likens it to murder (Matthew 5:21–22), and in Matthew 6:25–34, He also says we shouldn't worry.

There are also many things that aren't necessarily sins, but that the Bible advises against, such as debt (Romans 13:7–8, Proverbs 22:7, etc.) and gluttony (Proverbs 23:20–21)—we should exercise discipline in every area of our lives including our bodies and finances.

On that note, I wonder why so many Christians are so morbidly obese? In addition to multiple warnings against gluttony in the Bible, we should be exerting self-control anyway because it is a fruit of the Spirit. Furthermore, 1 Corinthians 6:13 (MSG) says, "it may be true that the body is only a temporary thing, but that's no excuse for stuffing your body with food, or indulging it with sex. Since the Master honors you with a body, honor him with your body," and verses 19–20 go on to say, "Or didn't you realize that your body is a sacred place, the place of the Holy Spirit? Don't you see that you can't live however you please, squandering what God paid such a high price for? The physical part of you is not some piece of property belonging to the spiritual part of you. God owns the whole works. So let people see God in and through your body."

So we should pay even more attention to our bodies than the unbelievers in the world, because we know it is the temple of the Holy Spirit. We have MUCH work to do in this department! We should not just act the part, but we should also look the part.

As I previously stated, I'm sure this is not an exhaustive list, but it is certainly a good starting point. If we avoid these things we should be well on our way to living a more Christ-pleasing life!

A Special Request for Pastors and Leaders

For the Preachers, Apostles, Prophets, and All Ministers Out There—Please Listen!

I realize this is a touchy subject, but please hear me out, as it is far past due and so necessary. Jesus's toughest words were for the Pharisees (the religious leaders), and so shall be mine. I will simply say to all: "STOP lying!" It is frustrating and confusing to your congregation, the general public, and especially "babes in the faith" when you preach to them about one thing, but then do another thing. You really do have to practice what you preach—if you can't do that, stop preaching, it's not for you. Have some integrity and stop being hypocrites. Acknowledge your shortcomings and failures, deal with them, and move on. At least this way we can trust you, and someone may get saved or delivered as a result of your testimony. But everyone loses when you just try to sweep things under the rug, and continue with business as usual. People are smarter than you give them credit for, you know.

Everyone already knows that pastors and other leaders in the church aren't perfect, so stop trying to make it seem as if your lives and everything you do *is* perfect! This just makes things worse when people discover your faults. Let the church *in* on your struggles and challenges—not only will you be more relatable, but this will encourage them in *their* faith!

Let's look at some of Paul's message to Titus concerning how church leaders should act:

> *Remember my instructions: an elder must be without fault; he must have only one wife, and his children must be believers and not have the reputation of being wild or*

disobedient. For since a church leader is in charge of God's work, he should be without fault. He must not be arrogant or quick-tempered, or a drunkard or violent or greedy for money. He must be hospitable and love what is good. He must be self-controlled, upright, holy, and disciplined. He must hold firmly to the message which can be trusted and which agrees with the doctrine. In this way he will be able to encourage others with the true teaching and also to show the error of those who are opposed to it.

For there are many, especially the converts from Judaism, who rebel and deceive others with their nonsense. It is necessary to stop their talk, because they are upsetting whole families by teaching what they should not, and all for the shameful purpose of making money.

It was a Cretan himself, one of their own prophets, who spoke the truth when he said, 'Cretans are always liars, wicked beasts, and lazy gluttons.' For this reason you must rebuke them sharply, so that they may have a healthy faith and no longer hold on to Jewish legends and to human commandments which come from people who have rejected the truth.

Everything is pure to those who are themselves pure; but nothing is pure to those who are defiled and unbelieving, for their minds and consciences have been defiled. They claim that they know God, but their actions deny it. They are hateful and disobedient, not fit to do anything good (Titus 1:5-16, GNT).

Verse 16 (the last verse of this passage) of *The Message* translation says it this way, "They say they know God, but their actions speak louder than their words. They're real creeps, disobedient good-for-nothings."

I bet few of you have ever preached Titus 1 in the pulpit! Why are preachers so insistent on covering up their sins, and the sins of other preachers? They have an alliance (I know, my dad is preacher, remember?) that often keeps them silent, and unaccountable. But don't you realize pastors are dying of drug overdoses and going to hell because no one will call them out? (These things really are happening—recall the story I told of the Floridian pastor earlier.) Don't you recognize that your ridiculous sins are modeling poor behavior, and that YOU will have to answer to God for leading innocent people astray?

Mark 9:42 (MSG) says, "if you give one of these simple, childlike believers a hard time, bullying or taking advantage of their simple trust, you'll soon wish you hadn't. You'd be better off dropped in the middle of the lake with a millstone around your neck."

And don't you understand that child molesters and rapists are being protected by people just like *you*? You are no better than those Catholic priests we abhor, and just as detestable as the Catholic Church that swept all the mess under the rug for so long.

Jesus said this concerning church leaders in Matthew 7:13–23 [emphasis added]:

Don't look for shortcuts to God. The market is flooded with surefire, easygoing formulas for a successful life that can be practiced in your spare time. Don't fall for that stuff, even though crowds of people do. The way to life— to God!—is vigorous and requires total attention.

Be wary of false preachers who smile a lot, dripping with practiced sincerity. Chances are they are out to rip you off some way or other. Don't be impressed with charisma;

look for character. Who preachers ARE is the main thing, not what they say. A genuine leader will never exploit your emotions or your pocketbook. These diseased trees with their bad apples are going to be chopped down and burned.

Knowing the correct password—saying "Master, Master," for instance—isn't going to get you anywhere with me. What is required is serious obedience—doing what my Father wills. **I can see it now—at the Final Judgment thousands strutting up to me and saying, "Master, we preached the Message, we bashed the demons, our God-sponsored projects had everyone talking." And do you know what I am going to say? "You missed the boat. All you did was use me to make yourselves important. You don't impress me one bit. You're out of here."** *(MSG)*

The Bible openly talks about good versus bad shepherds in Ezekiel 34. Jesus, the good shepherd, cares for His sheep (us), and looks after us, protecting and providing for us. On the contrary, the "bad shepherds" are described as greedy exploiters who will be doomed.

So preachers, have some integrity, please. When you mess up, just admit it, ask for forgiveness, commit to not doing it again, and keep it moving, stepping down if necessary (for more than just a few months) while receiving some counseling. And when you have been advised regarding a fellow pastor's sins, don't just get public relations involved to try to save face and let the man die—get that man (or woman) some help, taking them out of leadership to focus on their own salvation. Don't be a Titus 1:16 preacher—a good-for-nothing creep, taking advantage of your flock financially, emotionally, sexually, and etcetera. And most of all, don't just *talk* about it, **BE** about it.

For all of the good and honest preachers out there, this was not for you, but you know this had to be said. And to all of the dear people who have been scammed, manipulated, abused, or otherwise taken advantage of by one of these good-for-nothing losers (the Bible's words, not mine), please don't throw in the towel. Don't give up on Christianity altogether, but rather find a new church with a sincere pastor who can be a shining example of Christ's love.

Summation and Call to Salvation

In summation, there are many things God requires us as Christians to do. Paul sums things up quite well in Titus 3:1–2, 8–9, and 14 (GNT),

Submit to rulers and authorities, to obey them, and ... be ready to do good in every way. Tell them not to speak evil of anyone, but to be peaceful and friendly, and always to show a gentle attitude toward everyone.

*... I want you to give special emphasis to these matters, so that those who believe in God may **be concerned with giving their***

> **time to doing good deeds, which are good
> and useful for everyone. But avoid stupid
> arguments ... they are useless and worthless.**
>
> **Our people must learn to spend their time
> doing good, in order to provide for real
> needs; they should not live useless lives.**
> *[Emphasis added.]*

Another summation that I absolutely love is found
in Micah 6:8. The New Living Translation puts it this
way, " ... the Lord has told you what is good, and this
is what he requires of you: to *do what is right, to love
mercy, and to walk humbly with your God.*"
[Emphasis added.]

Lastly, recall 1 Corinthians 13:13 (MSG), which
was quoted earlier in this book: "But for right now,
until that completeness, we have three things to do to
lead us toward that consummation: *Trust steadily in
God, hope unswervingly, love extravagantly. And the
best of the three is love.*" [Emphasis added.]

So obey God and the laws of the government, do
good deeds, be nice to everyone, and live a life full of
love! These are the essentials for what it takes to
honor God and live a Christ-like life, and when you
look at it this way, it seems quite manageable!

It is my sincere hope that all non-believers who read this book, and all those who desire to live a life full of "fruit" will give Christianity a chance, and make Jesus the Lord of your lives. If this is your desire, just pray this simple prayer: "Lord, I confess my sins and renounce them all. Please come into my heart, and be my Lord and Savior." Once you have declared this, you are saved! Your next step is to find a faith-filled church, and grow in the knowledge of God, and get involved with helping others.

I hope that this information has been useful, and helps you as much as it has helped (and continues to help) me. I would love to hear about your thoughts, insights, challenges, and revelations as you walk with Christ! God bless!

Lord, I confess my sins and renounce them all. Please come into my heart, and be my Lord and Savior.

www.ingramcontent.com/pod-product-compliance
Lightning Source LLC
Chambersburg PA
CBHW021135020426
42331CB00005B/790